CONNECTING TO GOD

DAVE GATWARD

CW01102902

For Su, who helped me to believe in myself.

Copyright © Dave Gatward 2004
First published 2004, 2010
ISBN 978 1 85999 759 8

Scripture Union, 207–209 Queensway, Bletchley,
Milton Keynes, MK2 2EB, England.
Email: info@scriptureunion.org.uk
Website: www.scriptureunion.org.uk

Scripture Union Australia
Locked Bag 2, Central Coast Business Centre,
NSW 2252
Website: www.su.org.au

Scripture Union USA
PO Box 987, Valley Forge, PA 19482
www.scriptureunion.org

All rights reserved. No part of this publication
may be reproduced, stored in a retrieval system, or
transmitted in any form or by any means, electronic,
mechanical, photocopying, recording or otherwise,
without the prior permission of Scripture Union.

The right of Dave Gatward to be identified as
author of this work has been asserted by him in
accordance with the Copyright, Designs and Patents
Act 1988.

Scriptures quoted from The Youth Bible, New
Century Version (Anglicised Edition) copyright ©
1993 by Nelson Word Ltd., 501 Nelson Place, P.O.
Box 141000, Nashville, TN 37214-1000, USA.

British Library Cataloguing-in-Publication Data.
A catalogue record of this book is available from the
British Library.

Printed By Marsdon Book Services Ltd
Cover design: Hurlock Design

Scripture Union is an international Christian charity working with churches in more than 130 countries, providing resources to bring the good news about Jesus Christ to children, young people and families and to encourage them to develop spiritually through the Bible and prayer.

As well as our network of volunteers, staff and associates who run holidays, church-based events and school Christian groups, we produce a wide range of publications and support those who use our resources through training programmes.

contents

introduction	4
all in a day's work	6
out of bed	8
first lesson	10
what's it all about?	12
pressure	14
homework	16
life's ups	18
friends	20
holidays	22
feeling great	24
sense of purpose	26
sunshine and sand	28
life's downs	30
feeling low	32
bullying	34
what friends are for	36
can't cope!	38
doubt	40
panic prayers	42
the Lord's Prayer	44
exams	46
in trouble	48
what do I do?	49
scared	50
wake-up call	52
who is Jesus?	54
I want proof	56
dreams	58
eternal life	60
God's everywhere	62
nite nite	64
it's been a tough day	66
tired out	68
brain overload	70
what about tomorrow?	72
thanks for today	74
chill out	76
this weekend	78
music	80
forgiving friends	82
wow!	83
exercise	84
fast-food Bible bits	86
amazing facts	88
in the beginning	89
the Old Testament	90
Jesus' birth	91
Jesus' message	93
Jesus' death and resurrection	95

introduction

Pick any of the following words to describe what you think prayer is all about:

food friends thoughts worries future boredom holidays
weight image homework relationships parents death worry
pressure smiles sex childhood growing old shopping
the Bible learning music happiness brothers sisters

So, did you leave any out? No? Excellent! Because prayer is about chatting to God about life. And if that's the case, then there isn't actually anything that we can't talk about with our Creator. All we have to do is work out how to talk to him about our lives – not always easy! That's where this book comes in. And if you're ever stuck for an idea, if you're ever sitting there thinking, 'I wouldn't mind praying, but what about?' then check out the list of stuff that's running across the tops of all the pages. Easy!

So how else is this book going to help me?
Good question! As you read on, you'll find ideas and thoughts and questions to help you get praying. Prayer isn't something on its own but something that involves your whole life! Some of this book will work for you, some of it won't, but it *will* give you ideas on getting 'prayer' into your life.

Prayer's not supposed to be hard work and neither is this book. It's not something to read from start to finish or to study night after night, revise and then be tested on. Instead, look at it as a very useful coaster for that cold can of fizz on your bedside table! It doesn't matter if you spill stuff on it, write in it, draw in it, stick pictures in it. And it doesn't have to stay in your room, either. Screw it up and put it in your pocket. Leave it somewhere then find it later. Put it at the bottom of a bag. But wherever it ends up, whatever you do to it, if you find yourself sitting there thinking, 'Er… yeah, right, prayer… er…' just open this book and see if there's something in it to get you going.

ability · abuse · acceptance · accidents

all in a day's work

> So, son/daughter (delete where appropriate), what art thou doing on this fine and glorious day, hmm? Exploring the nature of the universe? Delving into the mysteries of the atom? Analysing the genius of Shakespeare?
>
> > Errr…
>
> Come now, does not the notion of learning excite thee? Tell me now what the day before thee holds!
>
> > Nothin' really, I s'pose.
>
> Pardon?
>
> > Nothin'. Just school. English and stuff.
>
> English 'and stuff'? What doest thou mean by 'and stuff'?
>
> > Just stuff, I guess. You know, PE and stuff. S'all borin' anyway. Rather stay at home. And our Geography teacher smells of cabbages.
>
> I beg thy pardon?
>
> > Nothin'.
>
> Well, I shall spend my day looking forward to conversing about thy hard day at school over tea this evening.
>
> > Yeah, whatever.

accomplishment · acne · acting · Adam and Eve

Here are some words about school. Circle the ones that describe what you think of school:

pressure	hard work	sandwiches	break-time
bullying	lessons	dull	homework
evil teachers	always raining	God	interesting
boys	doorway	friends	peer pressure
gangs	being cool	in trouble	faking illness
early mornings	breakfast cereal	kid's TV	late nights
no free time	girls		

Look over the words you picked – what do they show about your feelings towards school? Maybe school's going OK for you right now. Apart from some bad days, on the whole it's all right. You might even like it.

For other people, school doesn't exactly get the pulse racing. And no amount of being told 'it's good for you!' or, 'You'll regret it if you don't work hard!' makes any difference. The school's horrible, lessons are dull, the teachers are mad and homework is a waste of time. And then there's the getting up early, the rubbish bus journey, the late nights doing homework and the lack of time to hang out with your mates. Or something like that.

Now look at those words again. God's in there somewhere. Hard to believe, but true. No matter what you think about school, whether you're top or bottom, cool or not, God's interested. All that's needed is for you to let him know what's going on. Even if you find school dull, that doesn't mean God finds your life at school equally dull, does it? No. So let's spend the next few days thinking about an average day in your school life and how to get God involved. It's not as difficult as you think…

adoption · admirer · admitting · adolescence

all in a day's work
out of bed

The Lord called Samuel for the third time. Samuel got up and went to Eli and said, 'I am here. You called me.' Then Eli realised the Lord was calling the boy. So he told Samuel, 'Go to bed. If he calls you again, say, "Speak, Lord. I am your servant and I am listening."' So Samuel went and lay down in bed. The Lord came and stood there and called as he had before, 'Samuel! Samuel!' Samuel said, 'Speak, Lord. I am your servant and I am listening.'*

Get hold of a note pad and a pen. Leave it by your bed. This is your 'morning thinking stuff' pad. Decorate it in Dr Pepper stains and crisps and cheesy strings and stickers (some of these are optional). Every morning, stop and think for a minute about some of these:

    yourself   what's happening today?   lessons   homework
        mates   stuff that needs sorting   break-time
           someone at school   life at home

Write down whatever pops into your head about these things. It may be something you need to do, something that's on your mind,

*1 Samuel 3:8–10

adventure · afraid · afterlife · age · aggression

or something you feel good about. As the pad fills up, it'll be a massive help with organising your thoughts, and also give you a great starting point for what you chat to God about. Easy peasy.

Samuel's young and keeps getting woken up because something's bothering him. Something's on his mind, and he needs to sort it out. In his case, he's hearing God but thinks it's actually Eli. Ever woken up thinking of something that needs sorting out? What do you usually do about it? Why not use your 'morning thinking stuff' pad? But you don't have to leave it till the morning – you might forget it!

It's the morning and your brain's still tired. Ask God to help you focus on what's what, sort yourself out and deal with the day ahead.

agony · aims · alone · attitude · Amen · amusement

all in a day's work
first lesson

After three days they found Jesus sitting in the Temple with the teachers, listening to them and asking them questions. All who heard him were amazed at his understanding and answers.*

Right, you're in school, and whatever lesson is next, why not try the following:

Before the lesson: No matter what it's about or how boring and rubbish you think it is, decide that you're going to leave the lesson knowing something you didn't know before you went in.

During the lesson: Find that 'something you didn't know'. When you've found it, find something else. And stop looking out the window or at you-know-who!

After the lesson: OK, so you've learnt something – top job indeed! Now think about this – you've got something out of that one lesson that you wouldn't normally have done. And do your best to stop looking out of the window.

*Luke 2:46,47

ancestors · angels · answers · animals · anger

Great story this – Jesus nips off to the temple and his parents find him days later taking the lessons! OK, so you're not about to do this, but this story shows that Jesus thought learning was important. Think about it: he knew he needed to learn, to help him become the person God wanted him to be. So would you rather waste your time or become everything you possibly can? Do you want to live your dreams or throw them away?

Ask God to help you to not waste your time and instead to get stuck in and to get the most out of the day.

apostles · approval · argument · army · Ash Wednesday

all in a day's work
what's it all about?

A thief comes to steal and kill and destroy, but I came to give life – life in all its fullness.*

In the box opposite, draw a rubbish self-portrait. On the left side of your sketch, write all the things that you like about yourself, what you can do, your dreams. Then on the right side, write down where you want to be in ten years' time, what you want to have done, what you want to be doing.

Remember that LIFE means Live It For Eternity. It's not about becoming a film star or a surgeon or a pilot or a pop idol. It's about finding what your life is for, what you're good at, then living it to the full.

Get God involved. Let him know that you want your life to matter. And that you want your life to be an adventure, a tale to tell, a story to be proud of.

*John 10:10

athletics · attraction · awake · art · babies

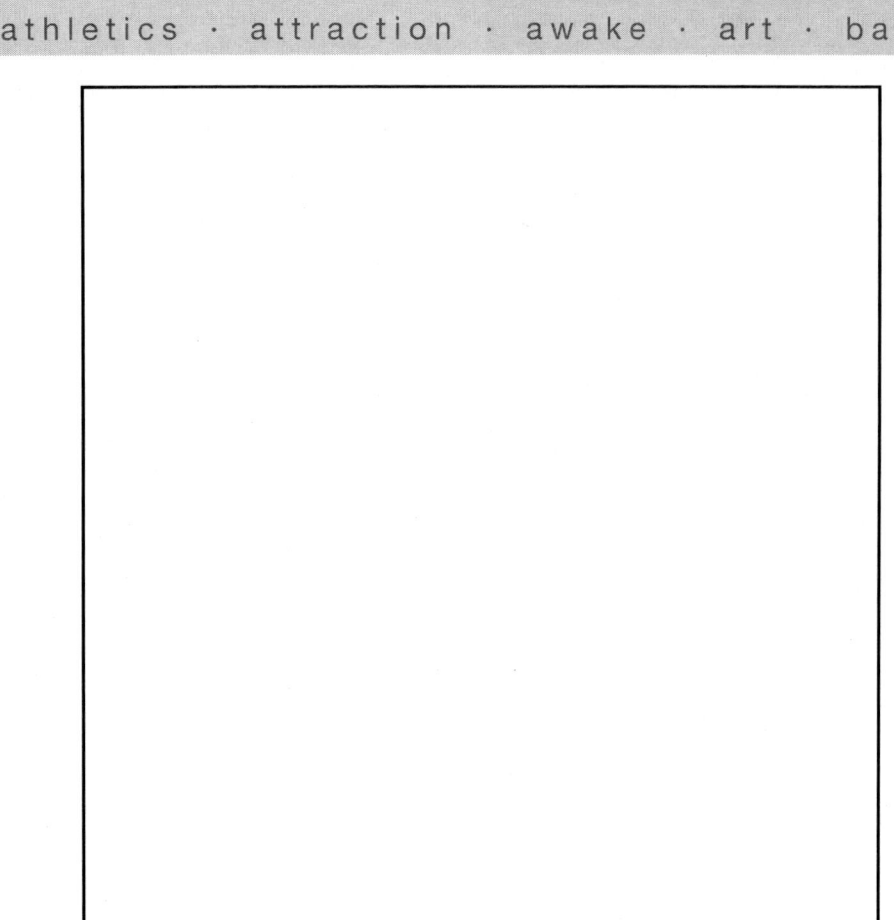

Bangladesh · brother · bank account · band · barriers

all in a day's work
pressure

Jesus got into a boat, and his followers went with him. A great storm arose on the lake so that waves covered the boat, but Jesus was sleeping. His followers went to him and woke him, saying, 'Lord, save us! We will drown!' Jesus answered, 'Why are you afraid? You don't have enough faith.' Then Jesus got up and gave a command to the wind and the waves, and it became completely calm.*

1. In the box, write or draw all the things that put you under pressure. Doesn't matter what they are – remember this is your book so write what you want. Some ideas could be: school work, trying to fit in, life

*Matthew 8:23–26

at home, girls/boys, body image, going along with the crowd, trying to please other people.

2. A hurricane is one of nature's most destructive forces – but just think about this: right in the centre is something called the 'eye of the storm'. If you were in a boat on the sea and in the eye of the storm, the water would be calm, the air silent, but all around you the storm would be screaming...

Hurricanes – sound a bit like life, don't they? Out of control, spinning round, knocking stuff all over the place. But what about that eye of the storm, the still bit that everything else spins around? Where's the eye of your storm, that little bit of calm?

Ask God to give you some calm in your life. Just when everything seems as if it's spinning wildly out of control, ask him to sit with you and be the eye of your storm.

belongings · benefits · belief · bereavement · Bible

all in a day's work
homework

And all those who have left houses, brothers, sisters, father, mother, children or farms to follow me will get much more than they left, and they will have life for ever.*

Homework timetables? Very silly indeed. But try something different – a life timetable. On a sheet of paper, write out what you do in one day, hour by hour (and don't forget the homework). Now look at it – are there any times in your day when you don't seem to be doing very much or perhaps just wasting time? Why not try some of the following:

cook   walk   learn something new

help someone   watch a favourite film   pray

read a Bible passage   phone a friend

talk to a relative   say 'sorry' to someone

try a new sport   play a board game with a mate

do some exercise

*Matthew 19:29

birth · birthday · black · blessed · blindness

Jesus is saying here that you have to give up a lot to live a real life. You have to put something in to get something out. It's easy to let time trickle away, to sit in front of a TV or computer and lose hours, days, weeks. What's difficult is to make the effort, to do something with your time, to sacrifice the easy way of doing things for something more worthwhile. After all, if you don't make time to chat to mates, you'll soon have no mates. And if you don't read the Bible or pray, where do you think your relationship with God'll end up?

Take time to get with God and to ask for his help to stop putting off important things because they're a bit more difficult than sleeping or watching TV.

blood · boastful · body · bombs · books · boring

life's ups

Son/Daughter! Come thou here and discuss with me why thy life is so full and so wondrous!

> Eh?

Come sit with me and we shall talk about all the good things thou doest that maketh thy life worthwhile.

> Sorry, I don't quite understand. You want to talk about why my life's great?

Indeed I do. For I do fill my life with gardening and collecting butterfly footprints. What, then, dost thou fill thy time with?

> Dunno. Just this and that. TV and friends I suppose. And school.

Come on! Think! What is it about thy life that doth make it tremendous? THINK!

> I can't.

Not an answer! Thou canst do better. Try again. I want to know what it is about what thou doest and who thou art that maketh thy life quite literally amazing!

> Er... OK... right...

Boxing Day · braces · breakfast · break-ups

Here's a picture of lots of balloons. Write something great about your life in each balloon until there are no balloons left. If you run out of balloons, draw lots more, all over these pages if you want – it's your book, remember?

It's sometimes hard to believe that life is great. The world's in a bit of a mess, there's drought and hunger and loneliness and hatred and … well, you know the rest. But life is good – or, at least, it's supposed to be. Trouble is, we often swap 'good' with 'easy' or 'enjoyable'. That's not necessarily the case. Life can't be good if we don't work at it. Life can't be good if we don't listen to Jesus and work out what we can really do with our lives. And life certainly can't be good if all we do is laze around doing nothing.

Want a good life? Want to live a life you're proud of? Want to be able to jump up and down and scream and shout about your life? Well, it's time to start really living!

life's ups
friends

Jonathan said to David, 'Go in peace. We have promised by the Lord that we will be friends. We said, "The Lord will be a witness between you and me, and between our descendants always."' Then David left, and Jonathan went back to town.*

Got a camera? Take a photo of each of your mates and stick them all to the back of your bedroom door. Every time you leave your room, you'll be reminded of them all and why they're so great. It's also worth remembering that they hang around with you because they think you're pretty cool as well. Nice to know, isn't it?

Write in the box opposite the things you think help to make friendship work. (I've included some examples to get you going.)

Do you make sure that all these things are a part of your friendships? Is God involved as well? Time to ask him to be…

*1 Samuel 20:42

brussel sprouts · bullies · burglary · calm

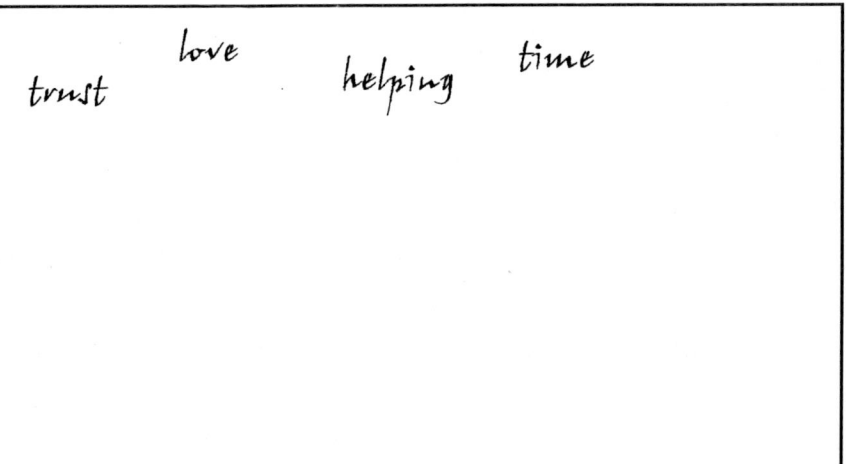

trust   love   helping   time

Focus on the words you've written in the box and ask God to help you with them.

candles · capabilities · career · careful · caring

life's ups
holidays

By the seventh day God finished the work he had been doing, so he rested from all his work. God blessed the seventh day and made it a holy day, because on that day he rested from all the work he had done in creating the world.*

Holidays include weekends, summer breaks, evenings off. A holiday is about relaxing and chilling out. It's also about doing something different with your time – from what you normally do all week. So start a holiday or time-off scrapbook. Write about what you do, take pictures, stick in sweet wrappers, information leaflets, leaves, anything. This book will remind you of how valuable it is to take time off. When it's full, start another one. Let God see it. Talk about it with him.

God created the world and then chilled out on the seventh day. How often do you chill out for a while? Or do you end up doing something else? All it takes is a bit of planning. Get all those things done that need to be done and try to make sure you have

*Genesis 2:2,3

one free day each week. Why is this important? Well, it gives you a much needed rest and it's also a way for you to say to God, 'Yep, I've worked hard. Let's spend today relaxing, OK?' And anyway, before you know it, you'll be chatting to God through your day off. Good, eh?

Everyone needs a break – even God! Ask him to help you work hard so that you can play hard too.

cause · century · certain · champion · chances

life's ups
feeling great

God looked at everything he had made, and it was very good.*

Jot down all the things you do that make you feel great. It could be stuff you're involved with such as sport or music, or favourite things you do with mates, or anything else that you just love doing.

*Genesis 1:31

change · chaos · character · charm · chat · chase

Now how often do you do these things? Are there some you haven't done for a long time? Why? How about getting them back into your life?

Ever get the feeling that you've no right to be happy? After all, there's so much that isn't right in the world, what have you got to be happy about? OK, so there are times when life is tough, when it isn't easy to be happy. But then there are other times when you feel fantastic about your life, maybe after you've done something great or experienced something cool. Remember – God created us to get the most out of life!

Sometimes prayer doesn't have to involve words. Thanking God is as much a 'doing' thing as it is a 'saying' thing. So next time you're doing something that makes you feel great, dedicate it to God.

cheat · childhood · chips · chocolate · choir

life's ups
sense of purpose

We pray that you will also have great wisdom and understanding in spiritual things so that you will live the kind of life that honours and pleases the Lord in every way. You will produce fruit in every good work and grow in the knowledge of God.*

Starting from now, see if you can begin to turn all those little things you do, as well as the big ideas for your life, into something that'll make God smile.

Our purpose in life is to make the best of every minute we've got for God. It doesn't mean everything you do has to be record-breakingly amazing. What it means, as it says in the passage you've just read, is that what you do each day should produce something fab for God. Now think about what you do every day from waking to sleeping, and see those things as a way of making God proud of who you are.

*Colossians 1:9,10

Christ · Christingle · Christmas · Christian · church

 Ask God to be there in everything you do each day.

life's ups
sunshine and sand

So God created the large sea animals and every living thing that moves in the sea. The sea was filled with these living things, with each one producing more of its own kind. He also made every bird that flies, and each bird produced more of its own kind. God saw that this was good.*

Most people like the seaside, but for me, perhaps the best bit is exploring in rock pools. It's not just toddlers in massive red wellies that do it either. No matter how old you are, it can be really cool to find some of the amazing creatures that live in rock pools. This planet we live on is stuffed to bursting with amazing creatures everywhere. God's creation is waiting to be discovered – so have a look around.

YOU are a vital part of God's creation! And you have the power to help make sure we look after this world, this gift from God. Try to think of just one small thing that you can do that will make a difference, that will make the world a better place. Ideas: recycle

*Genesis 1:21

stuff instead of just binning it. Find out about an organisation that helps look after the environment.

Close your eyes and think of the sea. Think of all the creatures that live in it, the billions of lives swimming out of sight. Thank God for his amazing creation.

complain · competition · concern · confession

life's downs

> Son/daughter, come hither for thou dost look perturbed.
>
>   Shove off.
>
> Thou art vexed, surely. And what is it that taxeth thy mind?
>
>   Leave us alone.
>
> Come, come, now! Lay upon me the troubles of your life. Let me help thee for I am old and wise and full of advice.
>
>   You don't understand!
>
> Of course I do! Share with me the wrongs that thou feelest.
>
>   And you don't listen, either! I'm going out!

Right, so life isn't always fantastic and brilliant. Sometimes you just want to ignore it or run away from it or slam your door and hide. Not all that useful, but when you're feeling down, it's hard to think of a more sensible solution.

In Genesis 9:16, we read, 'When the rainbow appears in the clouds, I will see it and remember the everlasting covenant between me and all living beings on earth.' Even when the world was flooded, something survived and good came from it. It's no different in our own lives, even if things do look particularly dark and frightening now and again.

confirmation · confrontation · confusion · conservation

Here's a graph to help you chart how you feel for the next two weeks. Copy it out so you'll have your own version that's big enough to scribble on.

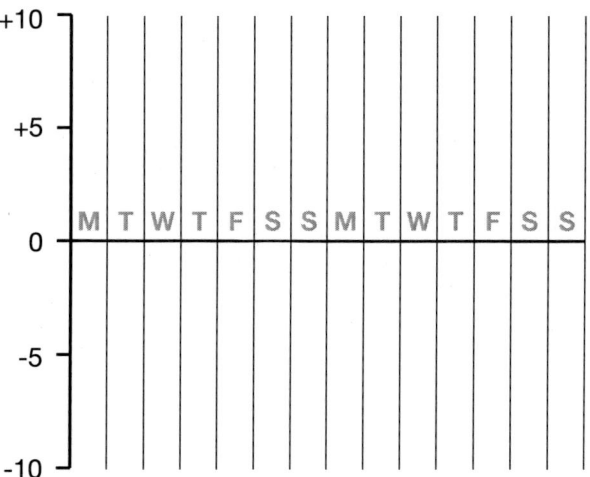

Now for each day decide how you feel: -10 is very low, +10 is very happy! As you do this, think about what's making you happy and what's getting you down. At the end of the two weeks, work out a way to get into your life more of the stuff that makes you happy – and less of the stuff that doesn't.

Is life supposed to be easy? Or is it supposed to be an adventure, involving ups and downs and highs and lows? Life can be difficult, but it doesn't have to be impossible. God's not there to make things easy and take away our responsibility for our own lives, but he's there to help, and to work alongside us as we grow.

conversation · cool · copy-cat · countryside

life's downs
feeling low

As Jesus was having dinner at Matthew's house, many tax collectors and 'sinners' came and ate with Jesus and his followers. When the Pharisees saw this, they asked Jesus' followers, 'Why does your teacher eat with tax collectors and sinners?' When Jesus heard them, he said, 'It is not the healthy people who need a doctor, but the sick.'*

What gets you down, makes you feel low? Write it here:

What makes you feel better? Write it here:

*Matthew 9:10–12

When we feel down, it's easy to mooch around in a mood, slamming doors and being grumpy. But what use is that? It doesn't help anyone else work out what's wrong, and it certainly doesn't help you. It's easy to say, 'Tell Jesus about it,' but sometimes we need something different. That's one of the reasons God gave us friends and family.

Sometimes, when you're feeling down, words don't come easily. But do we always need them? Probably not. God knows how we feel and sometimes all we need to do is just sit quietly and say, 'God, sit with me.'

crucifixion · cruelty · crusade · crying · Dad

life's downs
bullying

Two sparrows cost only a penny, but not even one of them can die without your Father's knowing it. God even knows how many hairs are on your head. So don't be afraid. You are worth much more than many sparrows.*

Pinch yourself! Go on! Now do it again! Hurts, doesn't it? But that's only pain on the outside. Bullying often causes pain on the inside as well. If you've been bullied, you probably know what it feels like. If you haven't, try to think what it'd be like.

But what's that got to do with sparrows and the hairs on your head? Well, bullying makes you feel rubbish, that you're not worth anything, that no one likes you. But it's not true! In fact, we're so valuable to God he's given us people who love us and can help. Praying might not solve things on its own, but could provide that little bit of extra courage you need to sort it out.

*Matthew 10:29–31

Nothing should be dealt with alone. That's what friends are for. Remember – you're so special to God that he even knows how many hairs are on your head!

> **If you're being bullied, TELL SOMEBODY you trust.**

This is a tough one – pray for those people who bully others. Think of the reasons why people bully others. Many of these things are down to the individual to sort out. Pray that they will do it soon.

decisions · defeat · dentist · depressed · detention

life's downs
what friends are for

The greatest love a person can show is to die for his friends.*

What would you do to help a friend? Think of times when your friends have needed help and you've helped them. Think of when they've done the same for you. If you've still got their pictures on the back of your door, look at them again and think how important they are and how much they help you when you really are feeling completely rubbish.

Sometimes it can feel as if it's our friends who actually make us feel rubbish in the first place! From time to time, we *all* say things that we don't mean and treat our friends badly. If this happens, try to make things better with the other person (even if you think it was their fault – hard, but it has to be done – Jesus says so). Then try to put it behind you. This *isn't* saying you should be a doormat, letting someone hurt you over and over again. If it keeps happening, you need to get some new friends! You need people who will help build you up, not keep putting you down.

*John 15:13

different · dinner · direction · disappointment

think

Real friends aren't just around for the good times – they stick around to help you get through the bad stuff as well. That's what Jesus did for his friends, the disciples – when they needed help, Jesus was there by their side. And of course, he does the same for us today. That's how amazing friendship is. Now think… what is it about you that makes you a good friend? Are there some things you need to change?

pray

Think of your friends and ask God to help you be a better friend. Maybe this will mean trying to be more patient, spending more time listening instead of trying to get your word in, putting your friend first, forgiving instead of carrying a grudge around… whatever it is, ask for God's help. The way we treat each other matters to him a lot, so this is really important stuff!

discover · discrimination · divine · doubt · down

life's downs
can't cope!

read

*The Lord is my shepherd;
I have everything I need.
He lets me rest in green pastures.
He leads me to calm water.
He gives me new strength. He leads me on paths that are right for the good of his name.
Even if I walk through a very dark valley, I will not be afraid, because you are with me.**

do

Ever felt that all you want to do is run away and disappear? Well, here's a creative use of that feeling – think of THE place on earth you'd run away to. The place you'd feel safe. Either describe it or grab some magazines and find a picture that shows the place you want to be and stick it in here:

*Psalm 23:1–4

think

Running away because we can't cope sometimes seems to be the only solution. But does it really help? It doesn't really solve anything, does it? The problem is still there. It may not be easy to face up to things and deal with them, but most times, that's exactly what we have to do. Life isn't easy, but if you have a look again at that passage, you'll see that God's with us, no matter what. Even if life seems difficult now, it doesn't mean it will be hard forever.

pray

Ask God to protect you and keep you safe. Create that place in your mind where you feel safe and meet him there.

earthquake · Easter · Eden · ego · embarrassment

life's downs
doubt

Jesus said, 'Come.'
And Peter left the boat and walked on the water to Jesus. But when Peter saw the wind and the waves, he became afraid and began to sink. He shouted, 'Lord, save me!'
Immediately Jesus reached out his hand and caught Peter. Jesus said, 'Your faith is small. Why did you doubt?'*

Sometimes our faith is affected by what's going on in our lives. Why do you find it hard to believe in God? Tick the boxes:

☐ Because I'm not happy at the moment.

☐ There's not enough peanut butter in the fridge.

☐ I've fallen out with my parents/friends.

☐ Something happened at school and I don't know who to talk to about it.

☐ I haven't had new trainers for three months!

☐ I don't quite understand a lot of the stuff I read about God.

*Matthew 14:29–31

energy · emotion · end · empty · encouragement

think

Some days you could probably tick all of those! The thing is, it's easy to believe we're the only person who doubts. Everyone else is fine, no problems. They know God very well, they speak to him all the time, they have no doubts. But that's not true. Everyone has doubts, everyone has wondered if this whole God thing is for real. What's important is that we don't run away from our doubts but instead face them head on and deal with them.

pray

Tell God about your doubts. Ask him to help you get to grips with them and sort them out.

panic prayers

> Son/daughter! Come here and share with me the prayers thou mutterest to our God.
>
> What?
>
> Share with me the words and phrases thou useth to converse with our Creator!
>
> Er, well, er...
>
> Bring to me, if thou will, the many ways thou meetest with God when life is full and busy, for thou art young and thy time is filled with so many things.
>
> True, but sometimes it's difficult to pray and—
>
> Difficult? How can prayer ever be difficult? Surely do thou not find it easy to reach out with prayer?
>
> Er, no, not really. I can't find the words or anything, and my brain's just so full, and there's so much going on, and I don't know what to say, and the words don't make sense, and...

Sometimes, the last thing you want to do is pray. You're stressed, busy, depressed, angry, upset. At times like this, your brain feels far too full to have space for prayer. But it's at times like this when we really do need to stop and chat to God.

excellent · exciting · exhausted · existence

Check out Numbers 6:24–26, which reads, 'May the Lord bless you and take care of you; may the Lord be kind and gracious to you; may the Lord look on you with favour and give you peace.' This tells us that God wants to be involved with us, whatever else is going on in our lives.

Jot down in this box all the things that make you feel you haven't time to chat to God (eg what makes you panicked or stressed or low):

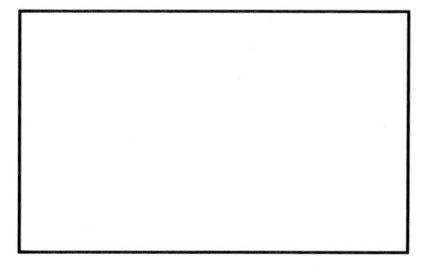

Now in this box, jot down all the things that make you happy, make you smile, make you feel that life's amazing:

Now every time you feel that life's getting on top of you and you haven't got time to chat to God, take a look at both of these boxes. In one you've got all the things God can help you deal with. In the other you've got all the things that make the low bits of life suddenly seem small in comparison. If life's getting you down, chat to God and he will help you. It may take some time but you're not alone.

Exodus · exile · expensive · experiment · extinct

panic prayers
the Lord's Prayer

So when you pray, you should pray like this:
'Our Father in heaven,
may your name always be kept holy.
May your kingdom come
and what you want be done, here on earth as it is in heaven.
Give us the food we need for each day.
Forgive us for our sins, just as we have forgiven those who sinned against us.
And do not cause us to be tempted,
but save us from the Evil One.'*

Why not try to use the Lord's Prayer as the basis for talking to God? If you use it as a pattern you'll soon find that you're praying about everything you need to. After all, Jesus taught us this prayer.

*Matthew 6:9–13

think

In times of trouble, it's easy to rush through prayer. But Jesus used this prayer to show us that if we just sit for a few minutes and focus on God, we can get our mind in order again. After all, most people find prayer difficult, which is why this prayer is so useful. It's a blueprint of how we should talk to God.

pray

Use the Lord's Prayer to pray about:

what's on your mind

the people around you

your friends

the world

faith · false · family · famine · fantastic

panic prayers
exams

read

So don't worry about tomorrow because tomorrow will have its own worries. Each day has enough trouble of its own.*

do

Right, stop worrying about tomorrow. Instead, do something about it. How? Well, why not write down a list of what you've got to do – then tick everything off as you get it done?

Stuff to do

*Matthew 6:34

far-away · farming · fashion · fate · favourite

think

This passage isn't telling us to forget about tomorrow and just get on with today. That's no use to anyone. What it is telling us is that worrying about it isn't going to solve anything. All it does is put us in a panic. Instead of worrying, we should get in control of what's happening today and work out a way of sorting it all out.

pray

Ask God to help you through tomorrow, no matter what happens. Exams aren't easy and you've got to do lots of hard work, but perhaps chatting to God will help you stay just that little bit calmer?

fear · feast · feelings · feet · fight · fitness

panic prayers
in trouble

read

Jesus rose up again and asked her, 'Woman, where are they? Has no one judged you guilty? You may go now, but don't sin any more.'*

do

How often do you feel as if there's a black cloud hanging over your head? When you've done something wrong and it seems everyone's getting at you? We all get into trouble now and again. What's important is what you do to sort it out. So, what do you do?

think

Grab your Bible and read the whole of this passage, John 8:1–11. Here, a woman is condemned by those around her, but after Jesus challenges them, no one can say anything else against her. All Jesus says is, 'Go, but do not sin again.'

We all do wrong things, but Jesus isn't in the business of condemning us for what we've done. Instead, he tells us not to sin again. In other words, accept you've done wrong, ask for forgiveness, then don't do it again. Simple and brilliant.

pray

Ask God to give you the courage to accept it when you're in the wrong and to do the right thing.

*John 8:10,11

flowers · follower · food · foolish · forgiveness

panic prayers
what do I do?

do

Enter through the narrow gate. The gate is wide and the road is wide that leads to hell, and many people enter through that gate. But the gate is small and the road is narrow that leads to true life. Only a few people find that road.*

do

I'll bet there's something you're doing now that's quite difficult to be really good at. You can't just do it by doing nothing, you've actually got to spend time and work hard at it. Well, don't give up! Keep doing it!

think

It's pretty impossible to achieve something by doing nothing. And it's the same with life. Following Jesus isn't easy – but although the path is narrow, it's the right one to take to have a great life that means something.

pray

Tell Jesus that you're going to stick with him and take the narrow path, even though it's going to be tough at times.

*Matthew 7:13,14

freedom · fruit · funny · future · gang · gasp

panic prayers
scared

One day Jesus and his followers got into a boat, and he said to them, 'Let's go across the lake.' And so they started across. While they were sailing, Jesus fell asleep. A very strong wind blew up on the lake, causing the boat to fill with water, and they were in danger.
The followers went to Jesus and woke him, saying, 'Master! Master! We will drown!'
Jesus got up and gave a command to the wind and the waves. They stopped, and it became calm.*

It's easy to get frightened now and again, just like the disciples in that boat. But remember: God is bigger than all of our fears. Need a reminder? Well, picture the sky at night, full of stars. If you can see the night sky clearly where you live, go and look at it, but if not, think about how huge the universe is, and how amazing our God must be to have created it.

*Luke 8:22–24

generation · generous · gentle · ghost · giddy

think

Feeling afraid is something that happens to all of us. It creeps up on us in all kinds of situations, making our stomachs flip and our minds go crazy. But as with everything, we are able to deal with it with God's help. And being afraid can be a good thing. If we didn't know how to be afraid, imagine the danger we'd get ourselves into and the daft things we'd do! Even fear has a place in our lives. And just like everything else, we have to learn how to accept it, all the time asking God to help.

pray

Think about those times in your life when you've been really afraid. Thank God that you survived them and ask him to help you next time you're afraid.

> **If you find yourself feeling afraid quite a lot, talk to someone you trust about it.**

wake-up call

> Son/daughter! Pray step thou forward and discuss with me our faith.
>
> > What?
>
> Let us explore what we believeth and come to a deeper understanding of what this is all about.
>
> > I'm not sure I really understand enough of it yet to—
>
> Fearest thou not! By exploring such deep truths, we can understand so much more, is this not so?
>
> > I guess, but I'm not sure enough about the simple things, never mind the really deep stuff.
>
> Deep stuff? But that is what this is all about! The depths of what we believeth! The truths we exploreth! The—
>
> > You really do go on, don't you?

Luke 17:33 says, 'Those who try to keep their lives will lose them. But those who give up their lives will save them.' This doesn't mean go out and jump off a cliff! Look at Jesus' life. What did he do that made him stand out? It wasn't only that he died and came back to life again. It was the way he lived his life.

Jesus lived his life wholly for the people he knew and met. It was an utterly unselfish way of living. Every waking moment was given to helping people, guiding them, and being with them.

If we only ever do things that benefit ourselves, where are we going to end up? Think about your friendships – you can't be a good friend if you only think of yourself, can you? So what we need to do is to be as selfless as possible in what we do. In other words, try to stop thinking about what we can get out of life, but instead, focus on what we can give. That's what Luke's on about and that's how we can save ourselves.

habit · hair · hand · happy · harvest · hate

wake-up call
who is Jesus?

read

God loved the world so much that he gave his one and only Son so that whoever believes in him may not be lost, but have eternal life.*

do

Write all the words you can think of that describe who and what you think Jesus is:

*John 3:16

heart · heaven · hectic · hell · help · heroic

think

Jesus was killed by being nailed to a cross made of wood. Do you believe he came back to life again? Think about the people who knew him – his friends and followers. They'd seen him die and knew that if Jesus' enemies had their way, they were next in line. They were scared for their own lives, they'd lost their leader and they were in hiding. Then something happened, something so amazing that they ignored the danger and started telling people Jesus had conquered death! Many of Jesus' friends died in the process. So were they lying? Did they risk their lives because of something they'd made up? Or *did* something amazing happen? Did they see Jesus alive again after they'd watched him die?

pray

Think about Jesus' friends, how they must have been feeling when they'd seen him die. Now think about what must have happened to them to make them tell others about Jesus and who he was. Ask God to help you understand more about what your faith is all about.

holiday · homesick · honesty · humanity · humour

wake-up call
I want proof

read

Then he said to Thomas, 'Put your finger here, and look at my hands. Put your hand here in my side. Stop being an unbeliever and believe.'
Thomas said to him, 'My Lord and my God!'*

do

Does God exist? Here are some questions that many of us want answering. Got any of your own?

- Is God real?
- What proof is there?
- How can there be a God when there's so much wrong in the world?
- Where's Jesus now?
- How do I know Jesus loves me?
- What's my life about?
- What's heaven like?
- Is there a hell?

*John 20:27,28

hunger · idea · identity · idol · illness

think

It's easy to demand proof. It's easy to dismiss something because you can't see physical evidence. And it's even easier to ignore the evidence around us. Want proof of God's existence? Then think of the world you live in. Think of the trees, the countryside, the sea, the animals and birds. Think of all the amazing things in this world. It's all a matter of perspective.

pray

Ask God to help you see him in your everyday life and to help you deal with your doubts.

imagination · importance · impress · improve

wake-up call
dreams

read

People can make all kinds of plans, but only the Lord's plan will happen.*

do

What plans do you have for your life? Is there something you really dream of doing? Well, why not write it down here? Now try to work out some of the things you need to do to make that dream a reality...

Dreams

*Proverbs 19:21

intelligence · interesting · issue · jail · joke

think

We all have plans and dreams about what we want to do with our lives. But it's easy to forget that an essential part of our plan should be working out what God thinks we should do. After all, he knows us better than ourselves, and he also knows what's best for us. So who better to ask about what we should really do?

pray

Get God involved with your dreams. Tell him about them, about what you would love to do – don't miss anything out.

journey · joy · judgement · justice · kind

wake-up call
eternal life

read

This body that can be destroyed must clothe itself with something that can never be destroyed. And this body that dies must clothe itself with something that can never die. So this body that can be destroyed will clothe itself with that which can never be destroyed, and this body that dies will clothe itself with that which can never die. When this happens, this Scripture will be made true: 'Death is destroyed for ever.'*

do

You could get hold of some cheap flower seeds, some compost, and some pots and grow some plants, following the instructions. If you want, record the growth of the flowers with photos or drawings.

think

Eternal life is pretty difficult to understand but it's what Jesus told us about. We may not know what life after death is going to be like but Jesus promised it to us and he isn't the kind of person who'd say something that isn't true. He's even there waiting for us. Wow!

*1 Corinthians 15:53–55

pray

Think about what heaven might be like. Ask God to help you understand it a little bit more.

lunch · law · leadership · learning · lessons · life

wake-up call
God's everywhere

When the Lord God first made the earth and the sky, there were still no plants on the earth. Nothing was growing in the fields because the Lord God had not yet made it rain on the land. And there was no person to care for the ground, but a mist would rise up from the earth and water all the ground.
Then the Lord God took dust from the ground and formed a man from it. He breathed the breath of life into the man's nose, and the man became a living person.*

Wait for a nice day then go for a walk with some friends or someone from your family, remembering to tell someone where you're going and when you'll be back. Look at everything around you, try to talk to God while you're walking. Why not pick up some souvenirs on your way? Some leaves, a bit of bark, a few stones?

*Genesis 2:4–7

like · live · lonely · lost · love · loyal · lying

think

The earth isn't actually very big if you compare it to what's out in space. And if you think about just how big space is, your mind will soon be spinning! We can't even begin to imagine how huge the universe is – or how powerful God is. But doesn't it feel amazing to know that this God who created everything is interested in you, too?

pray

Thank God for being interested in your life on this one planet among millions of other planets floating in space that he created.

nite nite

> Son/daughter! It is of the night so soon and another day hath passed, hath it not?
>
> Yeah, I guess so.
>
> Then come! Let us share with our Lord our day's activities!
>
> Pardon?
>
> Let us discuss the ins and outs of our day with our God. Let us tell him of what we hath done, what we hath experienced, what we hath achieved!
>
> Well, I'm not sure I've done that much, really. To be honest, it's been a bit of bad day.
>
> Then tell God thy woes, thy troubles.
>
> I'm not sure I want to. They're private, really, and I'd feel a bit daft.
>
> Such nonsense! God is interested in all that thou hast done and all that thou doest! Let us pray!
>
> Er... well... er...

So it's the end of the day. How's it been for you? Had a good day or a bad one? Looking forward to getting to sleep, or a bit afraid of tomorrow? It can be difficult to be in the mood to chat to God. You're tired, you're thinking about tomorrow, wondering about what you did today. And before you know it, you're asleep.

In Luke 5:16, we read, 'But he would go away to lonely places, where he prayed.' Jesus understood the importance of prayer, the need to be alone to talk to God. Throughout the gospels, we read about Jesus going off on his own to pray. And it's just as important at night before you head off to sleep as it is at any other time of the day.

Need something to focus on? Well, why not start out small and get bigger? The following box is divided into five. Each section represents one minute of prayer. So use this one as a practice example and put something you want to pray about in each box. Don't just think about yourself, think about the people around you, what tomorrow may hold, what you did today.

1st minute:
2nd minute:
3rd minute:
4th minute:
5th minute:

Now, for the rest of the week, why not try to make sure that you pray for five minutes each night, using the above idea to help you focus? After all, prayer doesn't have to go on for hours. It's not how much you say but what you say, that's important. And anyway, God knows and understands why you're tired. So why not have a chat before you drift off?

nite nite
it's been a tough day

He causes the sun to rise on good people and on evil people, and he send rain to those who do right and to those who do wrong. If you love only the people who love you, you will get no reward. Even the tax collectors do that.*

Get a sheet of paper. Write down on it all the things that have bothered you today, all the things that have made you stressed, annoyed you, upset you. Now read each one, saying, 'Lord, help me with this.' When you've finished, screw up the piece of paper and throw it away. All those things are now between you and God. It's time for some rest.

Sometimes it's easy to think that God should make our lives easier. We've had a tough day, and perhaps someone's been mean to us or upset us. Maybe we haven't done as well as we should have done. Maybe *we've* been horrible. At those times it's easy to think that God really should be on our side. Well, he *is* – but that

*Matthew 5:45,46

doesn't always mean he'll wave a magic wand and make everything OK. We have to take the bad with the good.

Before you go to sleep, try to find just one thing from today to thank God for. It can be the smallest thing – whatever comes into your head.

name · nationality · nervous · news · noise

nite nite
tired out

read

Come to me, all of you who are tired and have heavy loads, and I will give you rest.*

do

Every night this week before you go to sleep, give your body a good stretch. Do all the stretches very, very slowly, starting with your neck muscles, then your shoulders, then your sides and arms, then your legs. If you're not sure how to do them, why not find out on the Internet or at the library? Once you've finished, your body will be more relaxed and you'll have a much better sleep!

think

There's one good thing about feeling absolutely dead tired – you often only get that way by working hard. And if you're working hard, there's probably a reason behind it. Think about what it is you're working hard for at the moment and about how you'll feel when you've achieved it.

*Matthew 11:28

non-believer · nonsense · normal · nothing

Ask God to help you keep going, even when you feel you could just flop down and give up.

obedience · occupation · offence · offering · old

nite nite
brain overload

read

Jesus said to his followers, 'So I tell you, don't worry about the food you need to live, or about the clothes you need for your body. Life is more than food, and the body is more than clothes.'*

do

Wherever you're reading this, have a think about all the things you own. You've probably got CDs, DVDs, roller blades, a TV, games, lots of junk, trainers, clothes… It's a long list! How often do you find yourself wanting better stuff, more expensive things, or worrying that you don't have the same stuff as your mates? Is it really worth worrying about?

think

Isn't it funny how we fill our minds with so many things we simply don't need to think about? We get so worked up and worried that before we know it, we've forgotten about the really important things in life. We don't get our priorities right and instead, become obsessed with things that just don't matter.

*Luke 12:22,23

pray

Ask God to help you sort out your priorities and not fill your life with things that simply aren't important.

outdoors · outrage · overcome · overwhelmed

nite nite
what about tomorrow?

But I have let you live for this reason: to show you my power so that my name will be talked about in all the earth.*

Why not take a different look at tomorrow? Instead of worrying about things that haven't happened yet, think about how exciting it's going to be. What *could* happen? How could your life change? Now for some targets. Write down three things on these targets that you want to do tomorrow that in some small way will honour God. Keep it simple and choose small things you know you could do. For example: Be kind to someone. Show respect to your teachers and parent/s. Be generous with what you've got. Help someone out. Don't join in with gossip about someone.

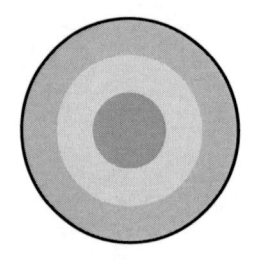

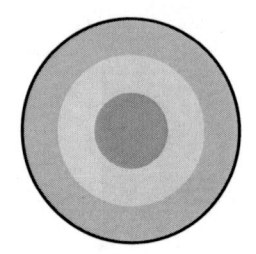

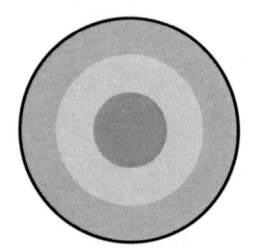

*Exodus 9:16

pain · parable · pardon · party · partner · past

think

We spend a lot of time worrying about tomorrow. But think how exciting tomorrow really is! You're alive, you've been given this gift to wake up and enjoy another new day. God will help you and use you to help those around you. Makes tomorrow seem a whole lot more interesting.

pray

Focus on those three targets for tomorrow. Talk to God about them and ask for his help to achieve them. Why not set yourself targets every night and give each new day something to achieve in God's name?

patience · peace · people · perfect · persecution

nite nite
thanks for today

Everything on earth, shout with joy to God!
Sing about his glory! Make his praise glorious!
Say to God, 'Your works are amazing! Because your power is great, your enemies fall before you.
All the earth worships you and sings praises to you. They sing praises to your name.'*

The psalms were written because people wanted to find a way to express their feelings to God. Some psalms were written during difficult times by people who were afraid, alone, or desperately sorry for something they'd done wrong. Many of the psalms, including this one, are full of praise for God. Why not write your own psalm, your own praise poem? Think of everything great about today, about why it's amazing that you're alive, and write it as a poem in the box opposite:

*Psalm 66:1–4

personal · personality · photograph · picnic

think

It's easy to forget to say thank you to the people we know and even easier to forget to say it to God. But just think about all that's happened in your life so far and all that could happen tomorrow. There's no excuse really, is there?

pray

Say thank you for as many things in your life as you can. Praise God for everything he's done for you.

chill out

Son/daughter! It is time to relax from the stresses and strains of this world! Come, let us rest ourselves.

> D'ya mind if I just listen to some music?

But thy music, it doth clatter and gnash in my mind!

> I could put the telly on?

But doest thou not find that this just wastes thy time and fills thy mind with rubbish?

> I think I'll just go and see some mates, then.

Doest what thou will, but make sure thou art fully relaxed for the week ahead.

> Whatever. Just chill out, yeah?

Chill out? What is this 'chill out'? I knowest not. Now I must take leave of thy presence. Goodbye, young person!

> Er... yeah... see ya...

poem · police · poor · positive · poverty · power

Chilling out, doing nothing, getting some time to yourself, relaxing, kicking back... Plenty of ways to describe it, and yet how many of us find it hard to do? We seem so stuck on filling our lives that we forget how vital it is that we step back now and again and relax.

So what do you do to relax?

Relaxing shouldn't simply involve grabbing the remote control and letting the day drift away. You can relax by just getting away from what you usually do with your time. That's why people have hobbies, or take part in sports. By relaxing with a purpose, we can actually learn new things about ourselves and how we deal with life.

Learning to relax is important but it isn't an excuse to waste time. Relaxing properly is about using time properly. It's about making the most of every moment we have on this earth, as well as giving yourself space to 'be'!

prejudice · pride · private · prize · prophecy

chill out
this weekend

read

So I decided it was more important to enjoy life. The best that people can do here on earth is to eat, drink and enjoy life, because these joys will help them do the hard work God gives them here on earth.*

do

This weekend, why not make a point of doing something entirely new? It might be just going somewhere you've never been before. It might be trying a new sport, watching a film you've never seen, eating something different… Whatever you do, see this weekend as an excuse to learn something! Whatever it is, make a note of it here as a reminder:

WEEKEND

*Ecclesiastes 8:15

think

It's easy to waste a weekend. Saturday morning becomes Sunday evening, then all too soon, it's Monday again. So decide to put your leisure time to good use by discovering some new stuff, and not just spending it being bored.

pray

Ask God to help you make the most of your time, especially the time you have to relax.

questions · quiet · race · real · rebel · receive

chill out
music

read

It is good to praise you, Lord, to sing praises to God Most High.
It is good to tell of your love in the morning and of your loyalty at night.
It is good to praise you with the ten-stringed lyre and with the soft-sounding harp.*

do

You might have noticed that there are lots of instruments in the Bible. People use music to praise God throughout the world, probably even in your own church. Ever thought about learning a musical instrument? Maybe you already play one – if so, have you ever thought about playing it to worship God? Try it!

think

Where would the world be without music? Where would our lives be without songs and tunes and dancing? Music can help us express what we feel, and it's a real way of enjoying and celebrating life. Whether it's banging a drum, twanging a guitar, or hammering out some jazz on a piano, music is vital to our lives.

*Psalm 92:1–3

redeem · reflect · regret · rejoice · relations

pray

Choose your favourite song from your favourite CD and listen to it while chatting to God. Thank him for music. Sing along to the song as well if you want!*

*Warning! Not all lyrics are exactly… er… appropriate to sing to God! Choose what you listen to wisely!

religion · remedy · responsible · revolution · right

chill out
forgiving friends

read

While Jesus was speaking, a crowd came up, and Judas, one of the twelve apostles, was leading them. He came close to Jesus so he could kiss him.
But Jesus said to him, 'Judas, are you using a kiss to give the Son of Man to his enemies?'*

do

If a friend upsets you or perhaps does something horrible on purpose, it's easy to be mean to them in return. We've all done it. But next time it happens, think about what Jesus would do – forgive.

think

What a moment for Jesus – betrayed by one of his closest friends. How must it have felt? Well, we all know to some degree because we've all fallen out with friends and it's not nice at all. But the only way to make the situation better is to forgive, as Jesus taught us to. After all, we all make mistakes, and there would be no hope for any of us if we were never forgiven for them, would there?

pray

Ask Jesus to help you not only to be a good friend but to forgive your own friends when they do something wrong or upset you.

*Luke 22:47,48

righteous · rock · rough · sacred · sacrifice · sad

chill out
wow!

read

Jesus said to his followers, 'Go everywhere in the world, and tell the Good News to everyone.'*

do

Fill the basin in the bathroom with some water. Let it become really still so that the surface isn't moving at all. Now let just one drop of water from a tap fall and watch the ripples. Amazing isn't it – one small drop of water causes ripples that reach the other side of the basin!

think

The way we live is a bit like that drop of water. We may think we're having no impact at all but think of the ripples our lives cause. That's how the Gospel spreads; by people like you and me living a life for Jesus and showing people just how great it can be.

pray

Ask Jesus to help you make the ripples from your life spread far and wide!

*Mark 16:15

safe · saint · sanctuary · save · school · scripture

chill out
exercise

read

Training your body helps you in some ways, but serving God helps you in every way by bringing you blessings in this life and in the future life too.*

do

Sport doesn't need to be expensive and it doesn't need to be something that makes you collapse with exhaustion! After all, rollerblading is a sport and so is using a yo-yo. So why not try a new sport yourself or with some mates? Here are some ideas:

tennis	rollerblading
running	football
walking	cricket
basketball	cycling (BMX)
ice skating	swimming
climbing	dancing
using a yo-yo	

*1 Timothy 4:8

think

If God's Holy Spirit lives inside your body, it's extra important to look after it. It's easy to be lazy but your body is one of the most amazing things God's given you so you need to treat it well!

pray

Thank God for your body and ask him to help you look after it.

fast-food Bible bits

> Son/daughter! Is not this Bible amazing? Doest thou not feel drawn to its wisdom?
>
> > To be honest, I don't read it much.
>
> Surely this cannot be so? How canst thou find not the time to read these words?
>
> > It's boring. Other stuff to do.
>
> These are words new to my ears! Thou wouldst find so much of value in its pages yet thou squanderest thy time on other pursuits?
>
> > I've no idea what you're talking about.
>
> Neither have I, but I knowest that thou missest so much.
>
> > Like what?
>
> Well, young-type person, why not have a look for thyself?

The Bible can seem pretty dull. Well, for a start, it's an enormous book. Actually, it's more like a library – a whole bunch of books – making up the Old and New Testaments. The thought of reading the whole thing from cover to cover can seem overwhelming! But who said you had to? If it's a collection of books, why not start with one or two and see how you get on? You could try Luke and Psalms, or Genesis and Romans. Give it a go!

Jesus knew how important the Bible was. He had a thorough understanding of what we now know as the Old Testament, and knew all its stories, heroes and characters. So if Jesus needed to know the Bible to understand more about God, how much more do we need to get stuck in?

spirit · spring · strength · stupid · success

fast-food Bible bits
amazing facts

The distance from the earth to the sun is about 150 million kilometres.

Light travels at about 300,000 km in one second. To travel to the stars we use 'light years' – the time it takes light to travel in one whole year – over 9,000 billion kilometres!

The nearest star visible to the naked eye is 'Alpha Centauri', which is four and a half light years away - that is, about 250,000 times the distance to the sun.

The sun is so large that if it were hollow, 1 million spheres the size of the earth could fit into it.

Our solar system is part of a galaxy called the Milky Way. Astronomers have estimated that there are at least 100,000 million stars in this galaxy.

The sun is just one such star. And the Milky Way is just one galaxy among many. There are at least 100 million galaxies in the part of space that telescopes can see. There are many more beyond.

suffering · summer · take · talent · tears · temple

fast-food Bible bits
in the beginning

read

In the beginning God created the sky and the earth. The earth was empty and had no form. Darkness covered the ocean and God's Spirit was moving over the water.*

do

Get a bit creative. Grab some pens or paints and a piece of paper and sketch out something which shows the world being created. It's not easy but think of all the colours and shapes you could use and try to think of a way to show God's incredible power.

think

God created the universe with his love – amazing! The world we live in and everything around us was made by God. Fab, isn't it?

pray

Think about one incredible thing you know about the world or one thing that you really love. Thank God for creating it.

*Genesis 1:1,2

testimony · text messages · thief · thinking

fast-food Bible bits
the Old Testament

read

Jacob lived in the land of Canaan, where his father had lived. This is the family history of Jacob.*

do

Here's a challenge... Think you know the story of Joseph and his rather impressive coat? Well, why not really try to understand it! Joseph's story is in Genesis 27 – 50. Try to read a little bit of the story every week, aiming to have read the whole story in a month.

think

The Old Testament is amazing! It's jam-packed with the adventures of cool characters like Moses, Samson, Elijah and David. There are tons of heroes and heroines, not to mention all the bad guys. And the wars and great escapes are real page-turners. So it's anything but boring!

pray

Ask God to help you get stuck into the Old Testament. Ask him to help you learn about some of the most amazing people in history and about their relationship with him.

*Genesis 37:1,2

fast-food Bible bits
Jesus' birth

So Joseph left Nazareth, a town in Galilee, and went to the town of Bethlehem in Judea, known as the town of David. Joseph went there because he was from the family of David. Joseph registered with Mary, to whom he was engaged and who was now pregnant. While they were in Bethlehem, the time came for Mary to have the baby, and she gave birth to her first son. Because there were no rooms left in the inn, she wrapped the baby with pieces of cloth and laid him in a box where animals are fed.*

OK, so you're probably not reading this at Christmas, but try to think about that time of the year. Which of these have anything at all to do with the Son of God being born on earth to save us?

turkey   presents   Christmas tree   candles

Father Christmas   shepherds   someone homeless

carol singers   Jesus in a manger

*Luke 2:4–7

unacceptable · understanding · ungodly · unique

think

The story of Jesus' birth is an amazing one. His mum and dad weren't married, they were in a town that didn't have room for them, he was born in a stable that was probably a cave, shepherds from the hills came to see him. There's even the story of the wise men from the east travelling to see him, and the story of angels announcing his birth… It marks the beginning of an amazing life as Jesus grew into the man who would show his people the way back to God. Why not read the story as it's written in each of the Gospels and really get to grips with the birth of Jesus?

pray

Ask God to help you see beyond the tinsel and presents at Christmas, and to begin to understand Jesus' birth and what it means to the world.

upset · vain · variety · violence · vision · voice

fast-food Bible bits
Jesus' message

read

(Jesus read these words from the book of Isaiah, the prophet. They had been written about Jesus many years before he came to earth.)
'The Lord has put his Spirit in me,
because he appointed me to tell the Good News to the poor.
He has sent me to tell the captives they are free
and to tell the blind that they can see again.
God sent me to free those who have been treated unfairly
and to announce the time when the Lord will show his kindness.'*

do

Why do you think Jesus came to earth? What do you think his message was about? Here are some ideas:

to save us

to heal people

to teach us about God

to experience life on earth

to show us how to live a good life

to live among us

to get to know us better

to die

to show us forgiveness

*Luke 4:18,19

vow · walking · warmth · water · weak · weather

think

Jesus' message is both simple and difficult. He came to save us, but from what? Jesus came to show us the way back to God and to help us understand the real meaning of love. He showed us this by mixing with people that others wouldn't even go near. He had friends and family. He healed, helped and guided people. He got angry at injustice and was happy when people listened to God's messages, understood them and then changed. Quite a person, don't you think?

pray

After you've spent some time thinking about who Jesus is and what he means to you, talk to him about your thoughts. Tell him how you feel about him. Enjoy spending some time with him.

fast-food Bible bits
Jesus' death and resurrection

read

When they came to a place called The Skull, the soldiers crucified Jesus and the criminals – one on his right and the other on his left.*

Very early on the first day of the week, at dawn, the women came to the tomb, bringing the spices they had prepared. They found the stone rolled away from the entrance of the tomb, but when they went in, they did not find the body of the Lord Jesus.**

do

Ask your parents or an adult you know to show you a six inch nail. They're huge, but nowhere near as huge as the ones that pinned Jesus to a cross until he died. But remember what happened next? Death couldn't even stop Jesus' message; that's just how powerful it is!

think

Jesus' message caused a stir. It frightened the people in power so they had him killed. And what was his message? To love your neighbour as yourself. To love God with all your heart, soul, and

*Luke 23:33 **Luke 24:1–3

you · yours · youth · zoo

mind. A message so powerful that even death could not beat it. So Jesus rose from death to show us that God's love conquers all.

But what about his followers? They probably thought it was all over. Their leader and best friend was gone, killed on a cross. They were probably next in line. All they'd believed in and worked for was finished. But they'd forgotten what Jesus had said. He'd told them that he needed to die to take away the punishment that's rightly ours… but that he would come back to life again. Who can blame Jesus' followers for forgetting this? So much had happened and they'd experienced so much pain – how could they ever truly believe that Jesus was who they had thought he was – the Son of God? But when Jesus did come back to life, he proved once and for all that death isn't the end and that there is hope for every single person who believes in him.

pray

Wow! Thank Jesus that he went through the pain of the cross so that we could have eternal life with him. Put into your own words how you feel about what Jesus did for you.